Not Quite on Grand Avenue:

Poems of the Early Years

poems by

Kim McNealy Sosin

Finishing Line Press
Georgetown, Kentucky

Not Quite on Grand Avenue:

Poems of the Early Years

Copyright © 2025 by Kim McNealy Sosin
ISBN 979-8-89990-050-1 First Edition
All rights reserved under International and Pan-American Copyright Conventions. No part of this book may be reproduced in any manner whatsoever without written permission from the publisher, except in the case of brief quotations embodied in critical articles and reviews.

ACKNOWLEDGMENTS

Thank you to the following journals, which published these poems, sometimes in previous versions:

"The Morning After He Left" in *Words in the Wind: Literary Anthology*, Nebraska Writers Guild
"Danger on Grand Avenue" in *Fine Lines*
"Of the Girls I've Been" in *Stories from the Heartland: Voices from the Plains Anthology Series*
"Ice Castle" in *Voices from the Plains, e/2*
"Minimum Maintenance Roads" in *Verses from the Plains: a Poetry Collection*
"Everyone Loves a Hardware Store" in *Words in the Wind: Literary Anthology*, Nebraska Writers Guild
"Meaning of Robins: A Tanka" in *Turkey Creek Preserve: A Sacred Journey* by Constance Spittler and Mary Bernier

Thank you to my Nebraska writing groups and to my poetry friends for encouragement and comments on these poems.

Publisher: Leah Huete de Maines
Editor: Christen Kincaid
Cover Art and Design: Kim Sosin
Author Photo: Photographer prefers not to be recognized
Cover Design: Elizabeth Maines McCleavy

Order online: www.finishinglinepress.com
also available on amazon.com

Author inquiries and mail orders:
Finishing Line Press
PO Box 1626
Georgetown, Kentucky 40324
USA

Contents

ONE
On Grand Avenue 1
Home Before Leaving 2
Childhood's End 3
Danger on Grand Avenue: a Prose Poem 5
Strawberries and Hawks 6

TWO
Not Quite on Grand Avenue 7
The House Between 8
The Apple Tree 9
War Lingers 10
The Morning After He Left 11
He Left: Mother's Voice 12
She Tried 13
Can Anyone Heal? 14
Don't Speak His Name 15

THREE
The Arranged Marriage 16
Stepfather: a Shadorma and a Tanka 17
Of the Girls I've Been 18
Unsung Childhood Talents 19
Ice Castle 20
Can This Be Love? 21
The Rocky Ride 22
Minimum Maintenance Roads 23
The Boy, the Lamb, the Lost Time 24
My Half Brother 25
We Kids We Lucky Kids 26

FOUR
Excitement in Town. circa 1957 27
Painting My Room with Mother 28
Everyone Loves a Hardware Store 29
White Corn and Red Tomatoes 31
Meaning of Robins: A Tanka 33
Open Me Up 34
Grand Avenue Reminisces 35
One More Bike Ride 36

ONE

On Grand Avenue

A gravel road along
    the edge
of a small town buries
    grit and red dust
into my memory,
looks peaceful, like
    a smile
that hides sharp teeth.

At four years of age
    I knew this:
the most ritzy road
in town
otherwise why
    name it
Grand Avenue?

Dad's gone to war.
    I hear
Grandpa tell Mom
    Dad fights
    panzer tanks
Battle of the Bulge.
    I'm scared.

Mom and I
live with Grandma
    and Grandpa
her mom, her dad
    We fight
fear and worry
    and wait.

Home Before Leaving

Dad, did I recognize you when
    you visited
    for just a minute
    after boot camp
before going off to fight?

During your training at Fort Hood
we had joined you, me at
    two years of age,
    while briefly living
in Temple Texas with other
families getting ready to wait.
No memories, just a photo.

Back in our small Nebraska town
only one memory of you lingers.
Handsome in your uniform, on the
    floral-carpeted floor
tossing my cousins and me in
the air to our giggles of joy.
    We had no idea.

Winter, 1942 with Parents

Childhood's End

If only I could have briefly
been friends with my
      grandma,
my mother's mother
when she was a girl.

Grandma was the oldest
of five at age eleven,
living in a one-room house
when her mother died
giving birth to the sixth.

So briefly a child
now a replacement
      mother
in charge of women's work
      laying the firewood
then sweeping the hearth
caring for five little ones
even working strawberry fields

for baking bread for breakfast
      when you had flour
cooking wild asparagus for lunch
finding a way to gather a meal,
locating scavenged potatoes
      gooseberries
for knowing edible morels.

I wish that for just one day
we could be children together
play tag, jump rope heel-toe,
play hide and seek with
    the other kids.
    And

I could say to you "well done!"

Winter, 1942 with Grandma

Danger on Grand Avenue: a Prose Poem

That day my friend and I were pretending to be wild horses, running around her large yard, horse-crazy little girls.

From the other side of Grand Avenue, Grandma stepped onto her front porch and called to me "Time to come home now, Kim. Right now please!" I took off, still in wild horse mode, galloping across the red gravel, but I forgot that the rule "Stop, look both ways, wait for the cars" must be obeyed by wild horses, too.

I will always see that huge black car kicking up red dust like a fire-breathing dragon coming too fast to see a small two-legged horse racing across the rocky road. Grandma shouted at me to stop but I knew I could run fast enough. Then my hoof skidded out from under me in the treacherous gravel. I went down, skinned knees and elbows burning, tears erupting from fright and pain, while the car kept coming in a swirling menacing cloud of red dust.

No time to think, no longer a horse, I curled into the tiniest ball. I could barely breathe from the dust kicked up as the driver finally slammed on the brakes, stopping with his huge silver bumper right above me. I tasted an acrid cloud, and after a moment of nothing I heard Grandma screaming and then felt her grab my arm. Grandma pulled me out from under the car, my bloodied knees dragging through gravel, voice whimpering. She held me tight, bloody knees, elbows, dust, and all.

These details reside permanently in my dreams. Over seventy years later, when something reminds me, my knees and elbows burn and my breath chokes in my throat.

Strawberries and Hawks
In memory of Grandma Nellie

On the side of Cemetery Hill
under a clear sapphire sky
    her tears come
    over a dual grave
    barely marked
Mother and Infant.

At eleven, she's the oldest,
now picking strawberries
    dawn to dark
    pocks her knees
    aches her back.
helps feed the family.

She sees shadows as
wings move, dark shapes
on the rough ground.

Wings on the dirt circle
she shields her eyes
    looks up
    red-tailed hawk
    her secret helper
she smiles, her garden guardian

and whispers *thank you*
    for your help.
No blue jays or mice dare be
  in my berries.
I can sell each box
    for one penny,
    buy milk, flour
for my brothers and sisters.

TWO

Not Quite on Grand Avenue

After VE day, he came home
    out of danger
    but like so many
    not the same.

Our own tiny clapboard house
    for the four of us
    my first bedroom
    gay daisy wall.

Baby brother, just in time
    to join
    the baby boom.

Not quite on that finest of
    gravel roads
    Grand Avenue

but down the street and around
    the corner, close but
    not quite.

Mother with Mike and Me

The House Between

Through the kitchen window in back
see the farm kids gather the eggs
sooie soooieee to the occasional pig
ride the horse, climb an apple tree
pedal bikes down unmaintained roads
    hike along the creek
    cap-pistols shoot bad cowboys.

Through the picture window in front
observe the small front yard, the 1930s
white wooden houses crowding both sides
the patch of mowed green weeds, all summer
hosting neighborhood ball games, kids
keeping softballs away from traffic
    kids breaking made-up rules, so
    seriously negotiated with friends.

My brothers and I grew up on this
    metaphysical soft border
not marked by lines, or fences, or rivers
but by a small house with a big yard
sitting at the thin intersection of environs,
the gradient meld of mental climes
kids grabbing life from both worlds
    the country backyard
    the town front yard.

The Apple Tree

No idea of the variety,
not sweet, barely edible
right from the backyard tree
grandpa might have
      planted.
Mom tried, made a pie
      apple plus sweet
      only once.

Each autumn, a few kids
      tried one
          ugh
the rest the tree threw away
      to the bare earth
no grass under that tree
      that squishy mess
      buggy, rotting,
attracting scary stinging insects.

Apples fell, as did we,
my brothers and I
each dropped more than once
from its tempting low branches,
knocking the wind out,
      gasping
      for equilibrium.

We were destined to climb
a few perilous trees
      growing up,
to challenge parental warnings.
But as was true of those
      bitter apples
      none of us
fell very far from that tree.

War Lingers

We thought they were happy, our parents, no shouting,
and in their quite different ways, perhaps they were
        from time to time.

Mom read to us, created stories to go with our picture books,
baked chocolate chip cookies, called her mother
        settled into family.

Dad sold hammers and nails in his in-law's small hardware store,
reliving, perhaps in horror, taking young men into battle
        against enemy tanks.

Quietly he was often dispirited, as were so many from this war,
chasing meaning in family, work, while craving adrenaline spikes,
        now and then creating them.

The Morning After He Left: Mother

Her coffee spill creeps across
    the breakfast table
    a relentless creek of mud.

Disoriented and decaffeinated
she fumbles to dam up the flow
presses her napkin like a dike
before the darkness reaches
    the edge

and drips to hell slowly
sinking all of her hopes for
    the years ahead.

He Left: Prose Poem in Mother's Voice

My husband left for good in the late fall. The day must have been cold. Our tiny living room had a chill, but not nearly so deep as the frost in the atmosphere. Kim, only six years old, stood on the metal heat register crying; Mike at three was there, too drowsy to pay attention. As much as it hurt to think of the children, the worse pain was knowing that we would have another child in three months, a child he would not know, would not help me raise. And as much as that hurt, the worst pain of all was knowing that he would be with another woman who was also having his child.

We three, he, me, and Kim, stood in that cramped room on that crisp autumn afternoon. The cold was seeping from the room into my spirit. We were all in tears, though I don't think Kim understood why. She only sensed that disaster was happening. I'm sure I was wringing my hands, clutching my apron, my housedress, angry, shocked, devastated, and I'm sad to say, begging. He stood by the door as though poised to leave quickly, tears in his eyes, but fear on his face. Agitated and disturbed. The other woman's husband was a hunter with guns and he was very angry.

My husband finally packed a small bag, fled from the room and out of our lives. I tried to keep my voice steady to reassure Kim and Mike that he loved us but had to leave. Kim asked, and then asked again, when he would be back and I tried to be honest: I didn't know but maybe never. I understood that this made no sense to her, and most likely at that point, neither child believed me. When I finally screwed up enough courage to tell my mother that he was gone for good, she was so angry that she swore we must never speak of him again. She never wanted to hear his name and never said it again in my presence.

Our small town, like most, had no therapist, though I would not have been able to share dirty laundry outside my family. My children needed to talk about their loss, but no one was there. I needed to talk about my pain, but no one was there. We were all too broken to know how to talk to each other.

She Tried

She tried tried tried
to help her children understand.

But they heard behind her words only
anger anger crushing anger.

He loved us but he had to leave
left us left left left us deserted

with no one nothing that morning
abandoned walked out walked walked.

Despite the hopes she tried tried tried
his last message hurt shattered crushed.

Can Anyone Heal?

What happens to children
when their father leaves?
I can't tell you much,
my memory was scrubbed
as soon as he was out of sight.

Their mother goes to work.
If the job pays enough
young women come in
to wash, cook, care for them.

In that tiny world behind
closed doors, eventually their
      crying stops, pain
      retreats, pushed
      deep inside.

The Three of Us

Do Not Speak His Name

How do you make a child forget?
Parse the pain from the pleasure
Pass over one, possess the other

Memorize the hugs, overlook the hits
Recollect the sunshine, reject the storms
Relive the arrivals, forget the leavings?

You might refuse to say his name
You might remove all reminders
You might hide all letters and gifts

You might succeed for a few years.

THREE

The Arranged Marriage

The marriage was arranged by the intended groom's pastor and the bride's father, a rural American Christian arranged marriage. The prospective bride needed help raising her children; the groom had never married, single and lonely.

This was no child bride event, no budding youth or fresh blossoming here; both were thirty-seven years of age, the woman had three children including an infant boy, a boy three years of age, and a daughter, seven. Her husband had abandoned them when there were two children and she was pregnant with their third.

The groom had never married, a lonely soul who took over land from his father. The hard-scabble farm was what was left after the deaths of his parents, who arrived from Germany at the beginning of World War I, and the death of his much older sister from breast cancer. For years, he lived alone in the shabby little farm house, no one to share or guide his life. But he was now willing to learn, to try to learn, to compromise.

Did they court as normal couples do? Only they know and (why does this always happen), it's too late to ask. But they did attend a church together, his—a country church, not hers—a small town church, until one Sunday morning his Pastor invited the congregation to stay for a marriage ceremony. Many did stay, but no one still alive knows what the assembled thought of this efficient wedding.

Her two sons—the infant and the boy— were there, too, but not her daughter, who lay in the hospital fighting pneumonia, praying her mother would remove that pink-veiled hat and go home —oh yes, dressed in their wedding finery, they stopped by. The girl begged to go home with only her mother and two little brothers, no husband, no stranger, just the original four of them again.

Stepfather: a Shadorma and a Tanka

Stepfather.
What could be so hard
for a child?
Replacing
the child's beloved father
with an imposter.

Consider
the man who never
had a child.
He is as
adrift as the child and feels
like an imposter.

Does a mother know
Who can replace a father?
This tells her the tale.
If the girl's crying becomes
"Please read me a story now."

Of the Girls I've Been

Of all the girls I've been
from sunrise of childhood
    to nearly sunset,
my favorite is that girl
    on horseback
in the glowing morning
    of age ten.

In that innocent season
my small town was beyond
    our front yard, and
a rolling country of grass
started at our back yard,
open arms waiting
to embrace us in
endless possibility.

Going riding with Janis,
announced as I slammed
    the back door,
off to saddle feisty Peggy.
Or maybe that day
all she needed was a bridle
    ride bareback
sunlight glowing our faces
    galloping out there
a perfect morning I thought
    would never end.

Mike with Me on Peggy

Mother through the window
    Be home by supper.
    Nothing more.
Not *Where are you going?*
    Don't go too far.
No freedom is as pure as that of
a ten-year-old girl on her horse
    on a day as wide
    as the prairie sky.

Unsung Childhood Talents

Look, Mom,
I say, in all innocence,
before loading up
an arrow in my bow
after practicing in our country
backyard all morning
and quite literally missing
the broad side of our barn
again and again.

But this deadly arrow
this murderous emissary
this bloody messenger
for the only time ever
flew straight and true
across our backyard
across my barbaric zeal.
I mourned her dead chicken
from my detention room.

Ice Castle

We knew no better
at ages ten and eleven, seven decades
ago in our rural plains town.

In the middle of a malevolent winter
both of us climbed onto Bonnie,
my friend's chestnut and white horse,
and urged her to a trot heading west
out of town past the cemetery.

Boarded in a pasture for the winter,
my horse Peggy thought her
cold weather duties were agreeable:
munch hay, grow a winter coat,
dream of warm green meadows.

Peggy's head snapped up at Bonnie's
clip-clop along the barely graveled road.
I caught her, saddled her, swung onto her back,
and we four crunched on into the cold,
our only goal an easy ride with a friend.

Our surprise hit quickly; a white-out blizzard
whipped into us and generated shivers of fear.
Soaked with snow and icy water,
girls and horses could barely see the road
through diamond-covered eyelashes.

Lost in churning white, shaking, then a miracle!
Sparkling and glimmering in swirling snow,
a radiant ice castle with a shining bell tower.
How could we have not known about
that glowing palace on this familiar road?

We opened the door to the empty freezing room
put the chopped wood into a pot-bellied stove.
"Welcome" decorated the chalkboard, still in use.
Frantic parents searched in the storm with no idea,
girls saved by rising warmth in a one-room school.

Can This Be Love?

What if you only *settle* for each other under family pressure?
What if arranged marriages are outside your tradition?

What if he comes from an austere world of all work?
What if she comes from a family of caring and love?

If his whole life was on a farm he'd nurtured for years?
If her whole life was in a town she knew by heart?

If he was active in a country Lutheran church?
If she was committed to a Methodist church in town?

If he had never been around children?
If she had three of them, one an infant?

If her family had a hardware store and expected him to help?
If his family, all gone now, left him a farm to care for?

Might they find compromises for so many differences?
Might he move to town and work in the store with her relatives?

Might they be married in his church after a Sunday service?
Might she give up her cherished church of dear friends to accept his?

Might he create a mini-farm in her country backyard?
Might she learn to preserve garden vegetables and meats?

Might she, after forty years, sit by him daily in the nursing home?
Might we now call this love?

The Rocky Ride

We each kept a pony on
the country side of our houses.
The summer she was thirteen
and I was close behind
my friend climbed onto Bonnie
and I onto my pony, Peggy
    both feisty
        as mares often are
nippy if you aren't careful,
a sunny morning with
warm south winds lifting
the horses' manes. Off to
    the rock quarry,
    our name

for our own secret riding place.
To get there, we had to urge
the horses off the old dirt road
across a small stream
up a rocky embankment
until we burst onto a
    hidden plateau
big flat boulders, a landscape like
that of the Western movies
    we devoured
at the local movie theater.

We were totally alone
    fledgling girls,
        anxieties hiding,
lurking. Huge rocks were
filled with crinoid fossils
we called "Indian beads"
rocks as treacherous to
the footsteps of our horses
    as each stride
in the nascent flowering
of two teenage girls.

Minimum Maintenance Roads
for Mike, 1944 -

With my oldest brother, three years younger than I,
    sitting beside me
I'm driving our parents' 1960 green Ford V8
crunching down tracks of crushed red gravel.
The car pulls a tail of billowing orange dust
on a new route between our small-town home
    and country church.

Our parents seldom left town, but for us, this,
our little frisson of travel in deserted places.
He spies the sign: "minimum maintenance road"
twin slashes in the dirt through a narrow opening.
"I wonder what's down those tracks?"
My brother and I did not, probably could not,
since the day we started to drive without parents,
    resist that temptation.

The more messy-scary-hair-raising the voyage
    the greater the adventure.
We've dropped into sloppy mudholes,
    "Gun it" he hollers.
We drove in tracks on an unstable rock ledge,
alternating dirty words with sort-of prayers
    "Oh crap! Oh my God!"
We've slammed the brakes, both screaming "stop,"
our front tires skidding onto a wood bridge,
    yawning missing boards.

Success meant not getting trapped, stuck, hurt,
    not being forced to back out
    yet just enough thrill.
No, not thrill, but awe, adventure, camaraderie.
I wish we could explore again, my brother and I,
rekindle our expired sense of teenager immortality.
To look down a lane of two suspicious dirt gashes,
    "I wonder what's down that road?"
And off we'd go, a last adventure, a quest
    for our once was.

The Boy, the Lamb, the Lost Time
for Jack: 1948-2023

Too seldom in our separate lives did we connect,
my second brother, six years younger, and I.

Not enough time among the fleeting days, with the only redhead
the image of Mother's father except for the errant hair color.

I recall gone-by days with him in a sequence of distant flashbacks.

Flash: In his top hat, he walks proudly with his lamb in the local parade.
Tears streak his face the next morning when his lamb lies ravaged by
dogs.

Flash: I ride in the front seat to church on Sunday, my brothers
in the back, whining *he's touching me!* Mom bites her tongue.

Flash: During church, he crosses his eyes at me and wags his tongue,
poorly suppressed giggles from both of us. Dad purses his lips.

Flash: From raising a lamb to selling cattle to owning a construction
company to cooking at his own restaurant. Like his Grandpa, a lifetime
of inventiveness.

Flash: Sneaks test bites as he carves the turkey for his beloved family
at Thanksgiving. I grin, his wife slaps his hand.

Flash: Lies in a hospital bed under a blanket of tubes.
    We all struggle for air.

Jack and the Lamb

My Half Brother
for Bill, 1951-1999

"It will not be easy to make this good.
Your life's brief blaze, in dying, mars the world."
from "For My Brother" by Greg Kuzma

Blue eyes from the prairie sky,
 Towheaded
completing our family set,
brown, sandy, redhead,
 blond.

Inside, outshined the sun.
 Smart, clever, funny,
mathematics was child's play
 infectious laugh,
but according to Mother
too often a "smart mouth."

As the breezy cliché goes,
he never knew a stranger.
You met him on a street corner
and you walked away convinced
that you had a new best friend.

Jack and Bill Each Catch a Fish

Yet thunderstorms loomed.
He inherited his father's farm
though not his father's work ethic.
A crop here, an illegal plant there,
everywhere, too much dreaming.

After a golden sunset
always comes the blue hour.
My brother,
such a luminous free spirit
could not be long sustained,
left us too soon in darkness.

We Kids We Lucky Kids

Fifteen people for dinner
for the midday meal
not just occasionally but
      every Sunday.
Ham or Roast Beef,
      or Turkey
      never fish
several vegetables, potatoes
fresh salads, dazzling desserts.

We took this, her, for granted,
we lucky kids, seven of us.
Grandma Nellie would cook
all night, then dress up,
      attend church,
come home to feed fifteen.
When Mother tried this
      rarely
her whole family worked hours
to create the spread Grandma
did by herself every Sunday.

We saw her rattled only once.
Grandpa decided on a surprise,
replacing her gas stove with a
      newfangled electric one
secretly on Christmas Eve.
      Christmas Day shock:
a strange stove, fifteen people
      expecting dinner.
The food was delectably hot but
the atmosphere was freezing.

FOUR

Excitement in Town. circa 1957

Fall: Friday night football under the lights sitting in the cold on splintery wood plank bleachers, wrapped in a blanket.

Winter: Tuesday and Friday night basketball, no girls allowed to play. Only junior varsity boys and varsity boys, several cheerleaders and an enthusiastic ear-popping pep band of mostly freshmen.

Christmas: Dress-up dance for school kids in the City Auditorium, now historic.

New Year: Local polka band, usually quite talented, fills the City Auditorium with athletic polka dancers of all ages. There is beer somewhere, but you might not see it.

Saturday Night or Sunday Afternoon: The local movie theater is probably showing a cowboy movie. For a quarter, get into the movie and maybe even buy a small bag of popcorn.

Summer Saturday Nights: The high school band plays on the bandstand in the town square park. Each player gets a dime following the concert. Afterwards, half of them go for ice cream or soft drinks. Others look for friends who are twenty-one.

Year Around: Find a friend with a car and drive around the town square ten times to see who else is doing the same. If it is summer and the swimming pool is still open, do an occasional lap around the lake and pool.

Year Around Over 21: Have a few drinks with friends at the American Legion Club. Then have a few more.

Year Around and In Love: Drive five minutes to the country, find a quiet dark place to, er, listen to radio music.

Painting My Room with Mother

As the child of a business family
whose hardware store sold paints
I was allowed to select my bedroom color,
no matter what unusual hue I picked,
then to help Mother paint the room.
She said *I know you'll be sensible,*
but just in case, she always diluted my
color choice with a double white base.

Orchid Dew pink covered those walls
for a few years, clashing with the red
decorations on my first desk.
Then *Chartreuse*—nothing complements
lemon-lime, not even an Elvis poster.
A few years later I went for *Lavender*
with a white chenille bedspread.
Quite girlie, never really *me*.

The togetherness of painting lasted
much longer than the color choice.
Mother and I rolled paint side by side
under no pressure for conversation.
How easy to share confidences
while not looking at each other, to carefully
edge around the woodwork, to cautiously
edge into and around life's intimacies.
Shared secrets brushed into pale walls.

Everyone Loves a Hardware Store

I cup my hands and peer through dirty glass
into our old small-town hardware store.
There, behind that window
the phantom of my stepfather, back bent in effort,
pushes, lifts, pushes the old wide broom
        maneuvers the oiled sawdust
down the worn wood pathway through laden shelves.

He two-steps with the broom to some forgotten tune
        moves from the front door to the rear
where the ghost of Grandpa relaxes in a rocker.
Yesterday, Grandpa showed his granddaughter
        how to repair a toaster,
imagines what adventures today might bring.

        Grandpa checks his pockets
        for a quarter
while he waits for his grandson to come in after school.
Grandpa, could you loan me enough for ice cream?
Gruffly, *Young man, do you think I'm made of money?*
        as he digs into his pocket
        pretends to search
for the quarter he already knows is there.

In the mist, I see the front door open and close.
        A customer?
Most made their hardware purchase early today,
headed to their fields or their jobs an hour ago.
I squint through the ghostly glass, recognize
        Grandpa's favorite crony in
        his gray *Kerns Hardware* shirt
from a job long ago, now quite stretched
with peek-a boo places between the buttons
        over his ample belly.

He claims the easy chair next to Grandpa's rocker,
sharing news, spreading rumors of who said what
        last night in Rick's tavern.
Grandpa remains alert for the door to open again,
a customer who might need penny nails,
eager to discuss the merits of
        a 16D nail for framing
        or a 6D headless for finishing
while letting the day wind down amiably.

White Corn and Red Tomatoes

On a sweltering Midwestern
    August day
we sit down for dinner
    corn-on-the-cob
    fresh garden tomatoes.
As I help myself, there I am
    not now but then,
a childhood family dinner,
everyone in appointed places.

Mother's red Formica table
Dad at the head,
    two of the three brothers
within his reach on each side.
I sit next to one brother while
Mom officiates opposite me
    next to the youngest.
My oldest brother at the foot.
We are in sharp focus, clear,
    hungry.

On many such summer days,
    waning times of
garden vegetables and strawberries,
we pick corn in the early mornings
    before the heat
    strip the husks
slide the white-gold cobs of grain
into a pot for exactly eight minutes
    while slicing
the cool crimson tomatoes.

"Pass the corn" brings me back
    quickly
today's baby white corn,
glass bowl of red luscious
    garden tomato slices.

Some of the same faces,
more lived-in now
but half of the faces who
had not long ago grinned at me
over the bounty of summer,
        departed.

Meaning of Robins: A Tanka

Fledgling messenger
first robin red-breast each year
brings tears to my eyes
missing you, mother, anew
remembering your magic
from one robin, you found spring.

Open Me Up

Fifty years of loving the city
yet open me up to find
visions of wide spaces in springtime
scent of white and pink wildflowers
blue rivulets flashing minnows
clip-clop of my spotted pony
breezes on a hot night in August
locust calls rising and falling
my spirit
soaring along a country road.

Grand Avenue Reminisces

My cracked paved road you see today, a palimpsest,
an overlay covering the richer grittier red gravel road
of my past.
I revel then and now in the attire, the regalia,
still around me.
The marigolds, the prairie coneflowers, black-eyed susans,
even wild asparagus.
My yards are green in spring, sometimes only weeds
kept mowed.
Perhaps a couple of my houses were even once
considered grand.

Indelible memories permeate my blacktop
of the family whose soldier son didn't come home,
of the boy who rode his bike back and forth
up and down
braved bloody knees to learn on gravel,
of the two teenage girls whose horses left tracks
along my edges each summer,
of all their childhood friends playing cops and robbers
in my ditches, trees, bushes and yards, then

of growing into teenagers racing their old broken cars
kicking up my red sand, before they
graduated with respectable records and went on to glory,
    or at the least, decent lives.
And of the unforgettable family who lived around the corner
close but not quite.
In the imagination of that girl
I'll always be the classiest road in town.

One More Bike Ride

Ride with me
       brothers
for one more time
       all of us
those who were
with us here
       and those
       half brothers
who never were.

One last bike ride
past our friend's
       yard
to the country road
the grassy airport
the moody stream
       a trickle or
       a torrent
between weedy banks.

Finally up the red gravel
of Grand Avenue
       one by one
off to our lives.